Mel Bay Presents

WESTERN SWING GUITAR STYLE

By Joe Carr

CD CONTENTS

1	Tuning Note [:17]

WITH BAND:

2	Sally Goodin 1, 2, 3 [:37]
3	Leather Britches [:28]
4	Durang's Hornpipe [:26]
5	Sally Johnson [:28]
6	Dusty Miller [:29]
7	Sally Goodin 4 [:28]
8	Chord Embellishment [:40]

WITH BAND:

9	Columbus Stockade Blues [1:07]
10	Cowtown [:32]
11	Wesphalia Waltz [:54]
12	Kind of Love [:38]
13	San Antonio Rag [:35]

14	Ballad [:39]
15	Blues [1:01]
16	Ida Red [:26]
17	Corrina [:29]
18	Beaumont Rag [:37]
19	Lily [1:09]
20	Sugar [1:03]
21	Time/Just a Closer [:36]
22	South [1:06]
23	Pipeline [:38]
24	Open and Closed Chords [3:52]

WITHOUT BAND:

25	Sally Goodin 1, 2, 3 [:37]
26	Leather Britches [:28]
27	Durang's Hornpipe [:26]
28	Sally Johnson [:27]

29	Dusty Miller [:29]
30	Sally Goodin 4 [:27]
31	Columbus Stockade Blues [1:10]
32	Cowtown [:36]
33	Wesphalia Waltz [:56]
34	Kind of Love [:40]
35	San Antonio Rag [:35]
36	Ballad [:39]
37	Blues [1:02]
38	Corrina [:32]
39	Beaumont Rag [:39]
40	Lily [1:15]
41	Sugar [1:07]
42	Time/Just a Closer [:35]
43	South [1:06]
44	Pipeline [:39]

1 2 3 4 5 6 7 8 9 0

Visit us on the Web at http://www.melbay.com — E-mail us at email@melbay.com

TABLE OF CONTENTS

INTRODUCTION

If you have ever heard the sound of rhythm guitar in a good western swing band, you may have wondered what the guitarist was doing. While the song might be a simple one with only two or three chords, the guitarist changes chords every two beats, providing a driving and harmonically interesting background for the singers and instrumentalists.

This book is designed for intermediate players who have a basic understanding of open chords. An accompanying video "Western Swing Guitar Styles, Volumes One and Two" (TX-60, 92G-15), which includes much of the material contained here, is available from Mel Bay Publications. The chords and progressions explained here can be used in many types of music in addition to western swing. The guitar style fits especially well with swing music of any type from the 1930's and 1940's.

If you haven't heard this style before, check out recordings by Bob Wills, Asleep at the Wheel and Johnny Gimble. Many of these recordings feature the great Eldon Shamblin, Bob Wills' longtime guitarist and the undisputed master of this style.

We will begin our study with what has been called the Texas fiddle backup style. The beginnings of this style are unclear, but it is my opinion that it was started by guitarists who heard and tried to copy the sound of Eldon Shamblin on the early Bob Wills records of the 1930's. Recordings of Texas fiddlers in the 1920's feature rhythm guitars played in the bass-strum pattern - the same pattern found on early recordings of southern Appalachian fiddlers. It is not until after Shamblin's first recording with Bob Wills in the mid 1930's that we hear the style on Texas fiddle records.

Special thanks go to Slim Richey, Alan Munde, John Hartin, Buster Redwine and Kim Fagerstrom for their help in my understanding of swing rhythm and the development of this project.

EQUIPMENT

Western Swing guitar music was originally played on the large hollow body electric F-hole guitars of the 1930's and 1940's. The guitarists used medium or heavier gauge strings. In recent times, most players, including Eldon Shamblin, use solid body electrics which are easier to carry around, more versatile and are less prone to feedback. The neck position pickup is used to get a fatter, more mellow rhythm sound. If you play several styles, you can still get a good swing rhythm with light stings. Some players, including me, beef up the bass strings in a light set to help strengthen the rhythm sound. I use a set that is .10, .12, .16, .30, .40, .50. This allows me to bend strings on the lead pickup on twangy country music and still gets a good swing sound on the neck position.

In the 1920's and 1930's, players like Eddie Lang, Django Reinhardt and Karl Farr recorded swing music using acoustic guitars. Acoustic swing music is enjoying a surge of popularity today. Almost any type acoustic guitar will do and many players prefer medium strings for good tone and volume. Providing good swing rhythm on acoustic guitar is hard work and takes strong muscles and well-developed calluses on the fingertips.

At Texas style fiddle contests across the nation, you will notice many guitarists with Gibson acoustic guitars. Their preference for this brand is similar to Bluegrass musicians' preference for Martins. Also unique to these musicians is their use of steel wrapped stings as opposed to the more common bronze wrapped strings used by most acoustic guitarists. Warning: DO NOT enter a jam session with a group of serious Texas Fiddlers with any of the following instruments: 12 string guitar, 5 string banjo, harmonica, autoharp. You may never be seen or heard of again!

SYMBOLS AND TERMS YOU SHOULD KNOW

Diminished = dim or o

Augmented = aug or +

Major   = Maj or M

Seventh   = 7

Major 7   = Maj7 or M7

Minor   = min or m or -

Sharp   = ♯ (one fret higher in pitch on the guitar)

Flat   = ♭ (one fret lower in pitch on the guitar)

Minor 7   = m7 or -7

Other chord numbers such as 6, 9, 11, 13 are self-explanatory.
example: G-13♭9 = G minor thirteen flat 9

TEXAS FIDDLE STYLE BACKUP
OPEN POSITION CHORDS

Also referred to as "Sock Style Rhythm", Texas fiddle backup features changing bass notes and chords, usually on every beat. The "Sock" comes from the percussive strum of the chord on beats two and four. A measure of this rhythm looks like this: 1)Bass note 2)chord, 3)Bass note, 4)chord. Texas guitarists use both open and closed chord forms and they often slightly mute each chord right after the strum to maximize the percussive effect.

"Sally Goodin" is an old time fiddle tune that had probably been a Texas favorite for a long time when Eck Robertson made his landmark recording in 1922. It is basically a two or three chord melody and is the perfect model to begin our studies. Here is the progression using three chords. Each chord letter represents four beats. Two chords in parenthesis get two beats each.

SALLY GOODIN 1

A	D	A	E		In Chord Numbers	1	4	1	5
A	D	E	(E/A)			1	4	5	(5/1)
A	D	A	E			1	4	1	5
A	D	E	(E/A)			1	4	5	(5/1)

Here is the music for a basic three chord rhythm for basic fiddle tune #1: "Sally Goodin", "Ida Red, "Grey Eagle", and "Tom and Jerry" all use this progression.

SALLY GOODIN 1

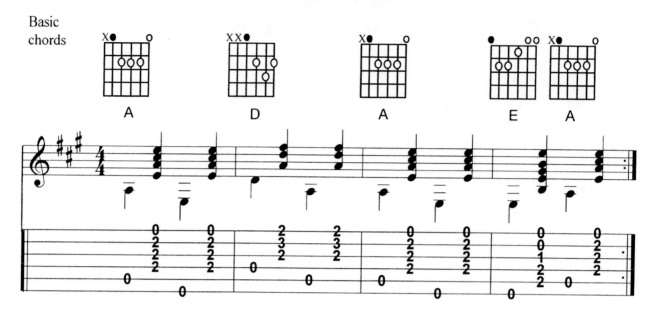

Pretty plain Jane. Let's spice it up a little by building our rhythm on this bass line:

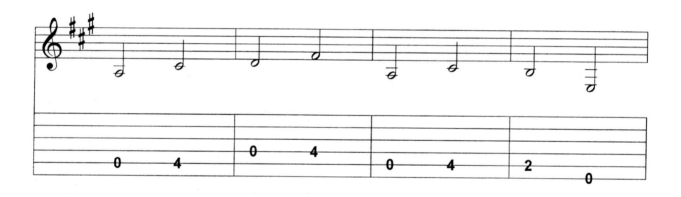

Now let's change our chords to incorporate these bass notes.

SALLY GOODIN 2

In the following example A/C♯ means an "A" chord with a "C♯" bass note. Each chord gets two beats. The chord chart looks like this:

				In	chord	Numbers:	
A	A/C♯	D	D/F♯	1	1	4	4
A	A/C♯	B7	E	1	1	2	5
A	A/C♯	D	D♯dim	1	1	4	♯4dim
E	E	E	A	5	5	5	1

The diminished chord will be used more as we go along. Think of them as "connecting chords." In these chord chart examples, play the lowest note of the chord (filled in) as the bass note on the first beat and strum the rest of the chord on the next beat.

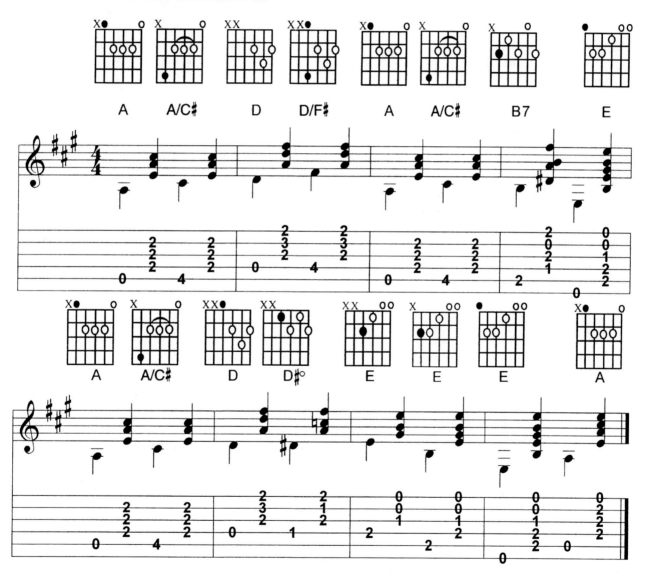

Let's play this progression one more time adding a few more changes.

SALLY GOODIN 3

A	A9	D	D#dim	1	19	4	#4dim
A/C#	Cdim	Bmin	E	1/3	b3dim	2min	5
A	A/C#	D	D#dim	1	1/3	4	#4dim
E	E	E	A	5	5	5	1

Notice that the D#dim chord connects the D to the E chord. This is a common use of the diminished chord.

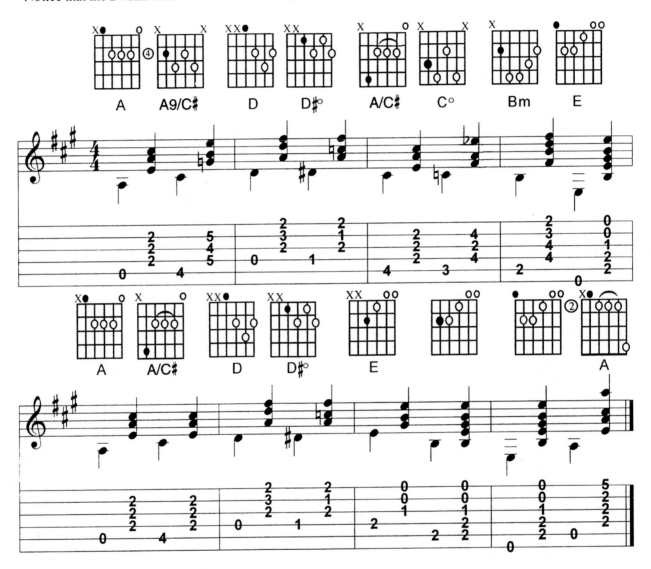

LEATHER BRITCHES

Let's try the same progression in the key of G. Tunes like "Sally Johnson" and "Leather Britches" use this progression.

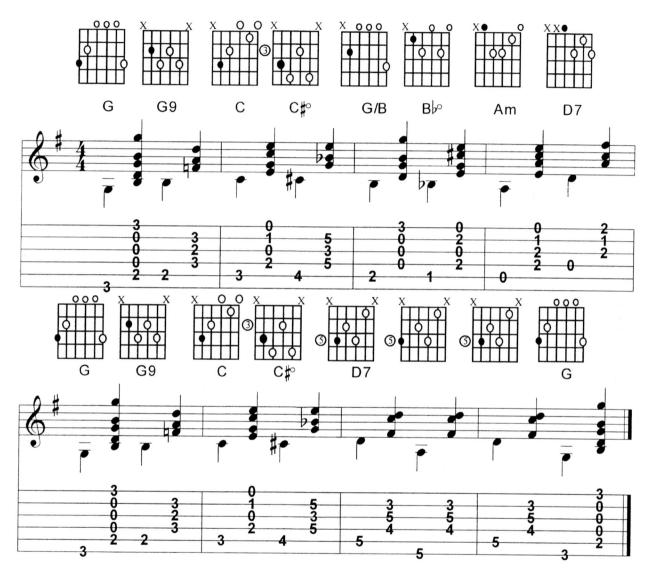

DURANG'S HORNPIPE

D is another popular fiddle key. Try this progression out on "Durang's Hornpipe" and "Sopping the Gravy".

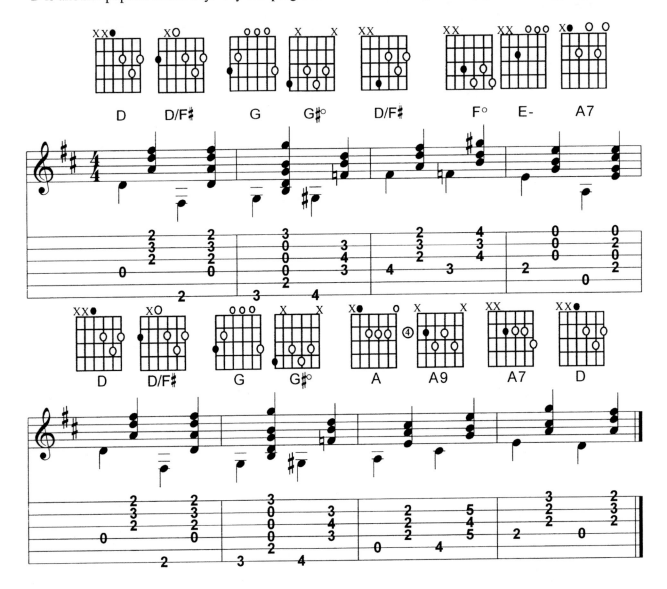

SALLY JOHNSON

Here is an arrangement of "Sally Johnson" taken from the playing of Robert Chancellor. Robert is a great Texas fiddle backup guitarist and brother of Texas fiddle legend "Texas Shorty" Chancellor.

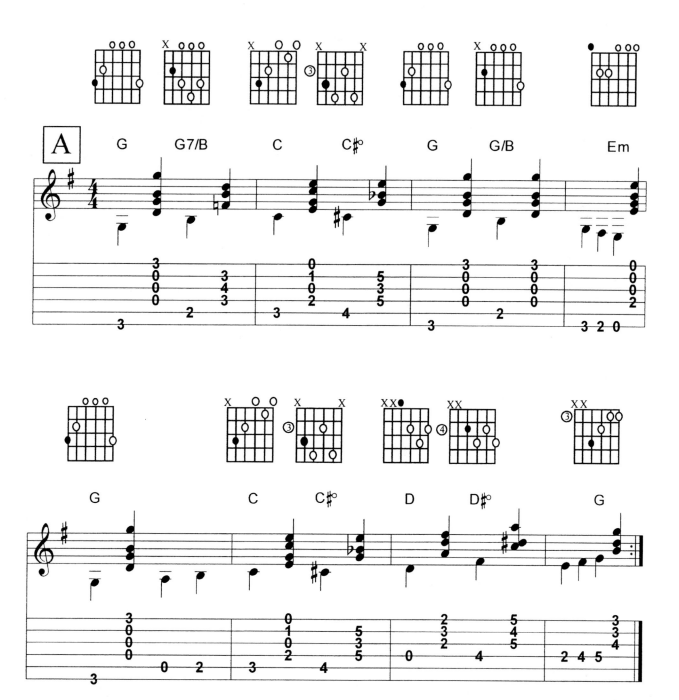

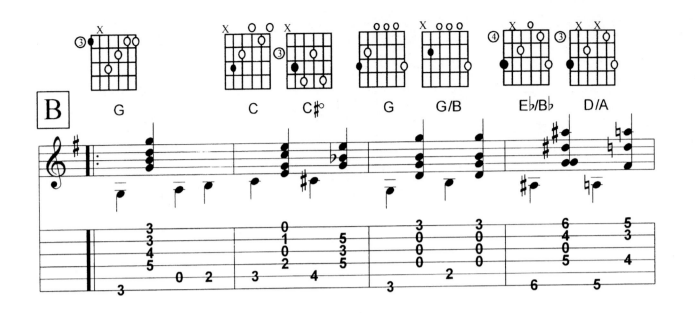

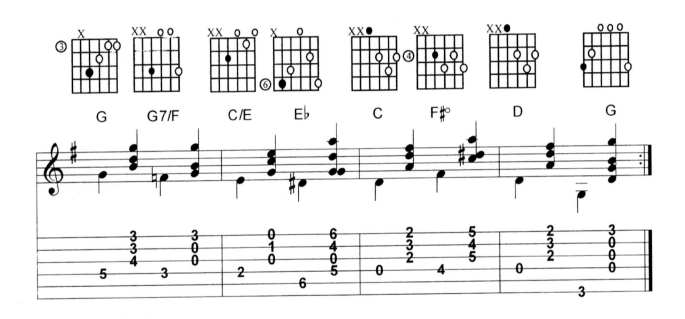

DUSTY MILLER

Here is an arrangement in the style of Bobby Christman who is a popular accompanyist on the Texas fiddle circuit.

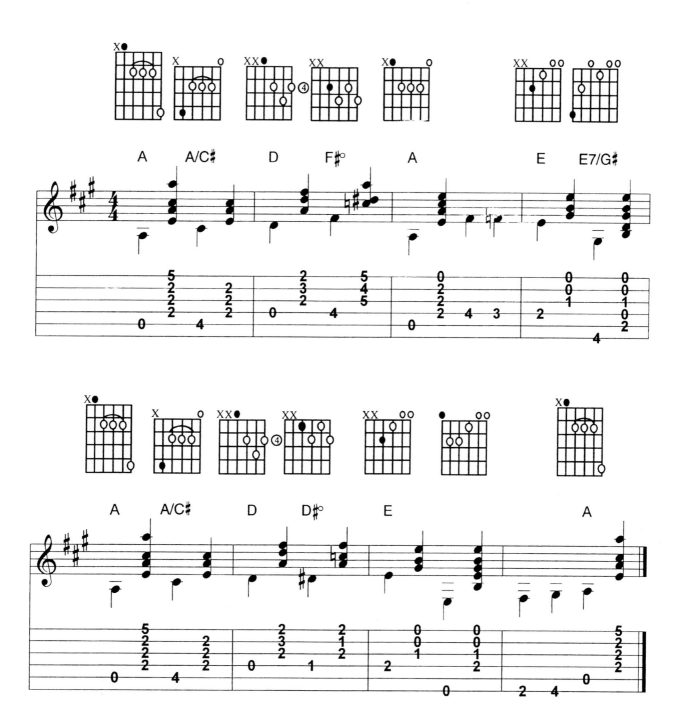

We can add a few bass notes and get this:

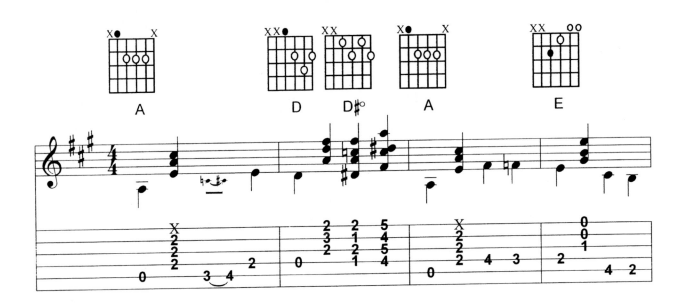

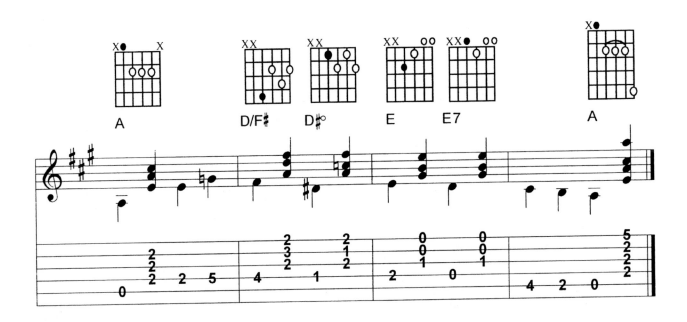

SALLY GOODIN 4

CLOSED POSITION CHORDS

Many Texas style guitarists use open position chords like the previous examples. Some, such as Royce Franklin, son of Texas fiddle legend Major Franklin, use closed position (no open strings).

We can play "Sally Goodin" using closed chords. Notice that this arrangement uses the same ideas as the earlier open chord arrangements.

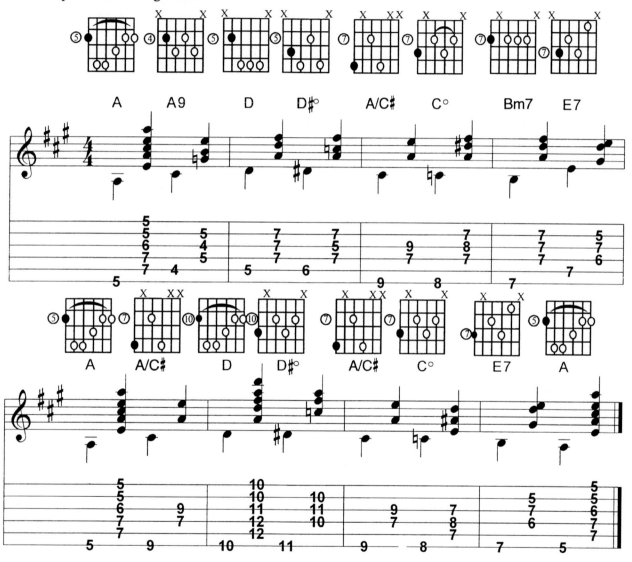

WESTERN SWING BACKUP

How is Western swing chord backup different from regular jazz guitar rhythm? There are many similarities and the same rules apply with this significant difference. Western swing guitarists do not usually extend their chords with the upper altered intervals that jazzers might use. Where a jazzer might play a D7 chord with a 13 or a flatted 9, the Western swing player might choose to play a simple 7th chord that would allow the instrumentalist the maximum freedom in his solo.

If the rhythm chart indicates an 7♭9 chord, for example, the soloist has fewer note choices that will sound "right". By playing a simple dominant 7th chord, the western swing rhythm guitarist leaves more room for the soloist and lessens the likelihood that what he plays will clash with the chords of other rhythm instruments, such as piano.

If all this sounds like gibberish to you, ignore it for now. Play the examples and enjoy the music. The emphasis in this book is what to play, not so much why. If you want a deeper understanding of chord theory, consult a good music theory book.

A Chord

SWING RHYTHM

The classic swing rhythm is a syncopated beat with a heavy pulse. Begin by making a standard "A" barre chord at the fifth fret. Play the A note note on the sixth string on the first beat. Now quickly strum the rest of the "A" chord and then release the pressure of your left-hand fingers on the strings. Be sure not to remove your fingers from the strings. Now repeat. The idea is to get a clear bass note followed by a very short chord. Practice this "long-short, long-short" rhythm until it is comfortable. You may notice your left forearm alternately bulging as you "squeeze-release, squeeze-release." A variation on this pattern is to strum the full chord on the first beat, let it ring and follow it with the shortened chord on the second beat.   Try this exercise to get the right feel.

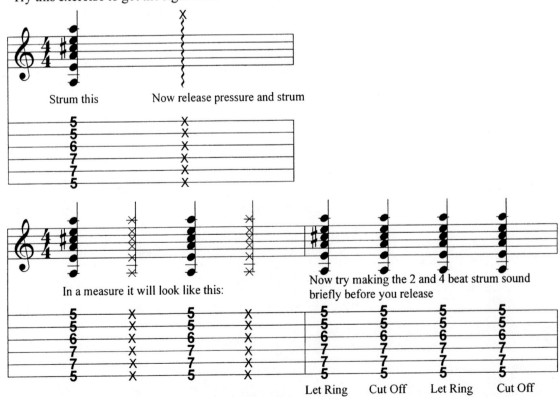

16

CHORD EMBELLISHMENTS

Another feature of western swing is that the chord progressions are often very simple. It is left up to the guitarist to "dress up" or embellish the chords. Let's look at a simple progression that would fit a song like "Columbus Stockade Blues."

Verse	1	1	1	1		Chorus	4	4	1	1
	5	5	1	1			4	4	1	5
	1	1	1	1			1	1	1	1
	5	5	1	1			5	5	1	1

Notice that the first line of the verse is all 1! This is 16 beats of the 1 chord. Let's look at what we can do.

Substitution Rule #1: Major equals major. What does that mean? Well, let's think of the key of G. Gmaj, Gmaj7, G6 and Gmaj9 are all major chords. (There are more than this, but let's use only these for now) Rule #1 says we can use any of these chords (if we like the sound) in the place of a straight G chord. So let's learn Gmaj, Gmaj7, G6 in one form. We could play 16 beats of G like this:

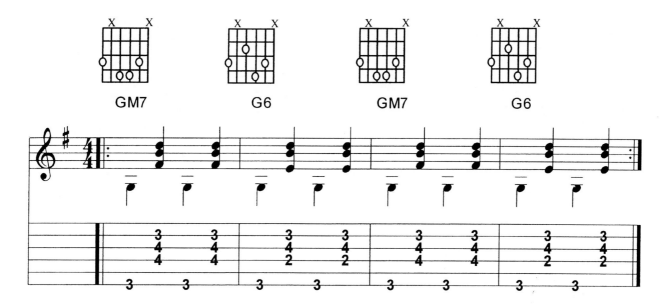

Or change the chords twice as fast:

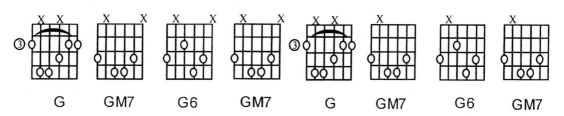

17

Now we are ready for line two of the verse: 5   5   1   1
This brings us to:

Substitution Rule #2: For any dominant chord, substitute a minor chord built on the 5th of the domi-nant. What? Stay with me and you'll see. First, what is a dominant chord? Without getting too techni-cal, dominant chords are restless chords that want to resolve to another chord. D7 is a dominant chord and it "wants" to resolve to G. Try playing D7 to G several times. See what I mean? So if D7 is a dominant chord, let's try rule #2 on it. First let's find the fifth of the D7 chord. There are several ways to do this. One is to memorize that A is the fifth of a D chord or you could count as you play down a D scale. I prefer to use a third method, using relationships on the neck. Look at the D7 chord.

D7

    Now move your third finger across to the sixth string. This note is the fifth of the chord and this is true for every chord in this shape all over the neck.

    Now we have found the fifth of the D7 chord (it's an A note). Let's finish applying the rule. Build a minor chord on the A note. It looks like this:

Remember this relationship. When you have this shape of a 7th chord, the minor substitution will always be here:

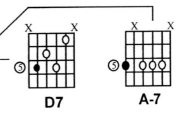

D7   **A-7**

This   Becomes this

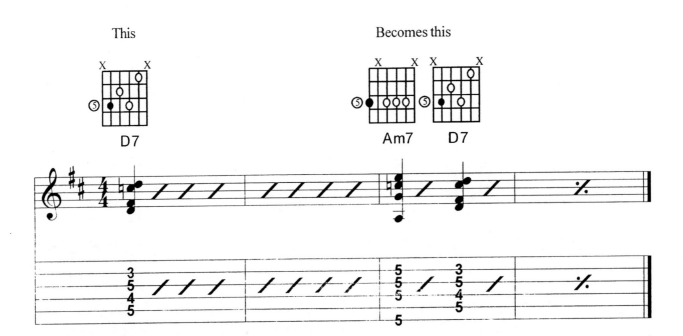

18

So let's put this in our song. The next two lines of the verse are the same as the first two so we can repeat our ideas until the last measure of 1. Look ahead to the chorus and realize that we are moving towards a 4 chord.

Rule#3:　　To move from a 1 to a 4 chord use a 1 dominant 7 chord. In our song, we can use a G7 to move to C. The chorus begins with two measures of 4 followed by two measures of 1. Time for our next rule.

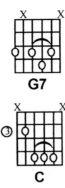

G7

C

Rule #4:　　To move from a 4 to a 1 chord, use a ♯4 diminished chord. In our song this would be C, C♯dim, G. In practice some players might opt to use the diminished chord for the last two beats of the second measure rather than for the whole measure. It would look like this: C, (C/C♯dim), G. This means you only play one bass note and one chord strum for the diminished chord. Let's apply all we have learned to the Blues and play this arrangement.

Verse

G	/	GM7	/	G6	/	GM7	/
G	/	GM7	/	G6	/	G♯dim	/
A-7	/	D7	/	A-7	/	D7	/
G	/	G♯dim	/	A-7	/	D7	/

G	/	GM7	/	G6	/	GM7	/
G	/	GM7	/	G6	/	G♯dim	/
A-7	/	A-7	/	D7	/	D7	/
G	/	G	/	G7	/	G7	/

Chorus

C	/	C	/	C	/	C♯dim	/
G	/	G	/	G7	/	G7	/
C	/	C	/	C	/	C♯dim	/
D7	/	D7	/	A-7	/	D7	/

Notice that I connected the "G" chord in the 14th measure to the A-7 chord with a G♯ diminished. This is another example of the connecting nature of diminished chords. Also notice line four of the verse. This pattern (1, ♯1dim, 2m, 5) is a common one in swing and jazz music. We will call it a "turnaround" because it does exactly that. It can be used as it is here or it can be repeated indefinitely as a "vamp" to introduce a song.

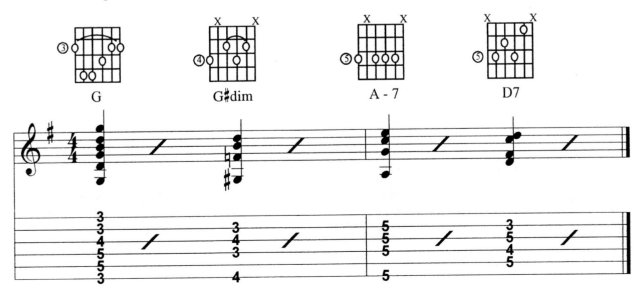

COLUMBUS STOCKADE

with all substitutions

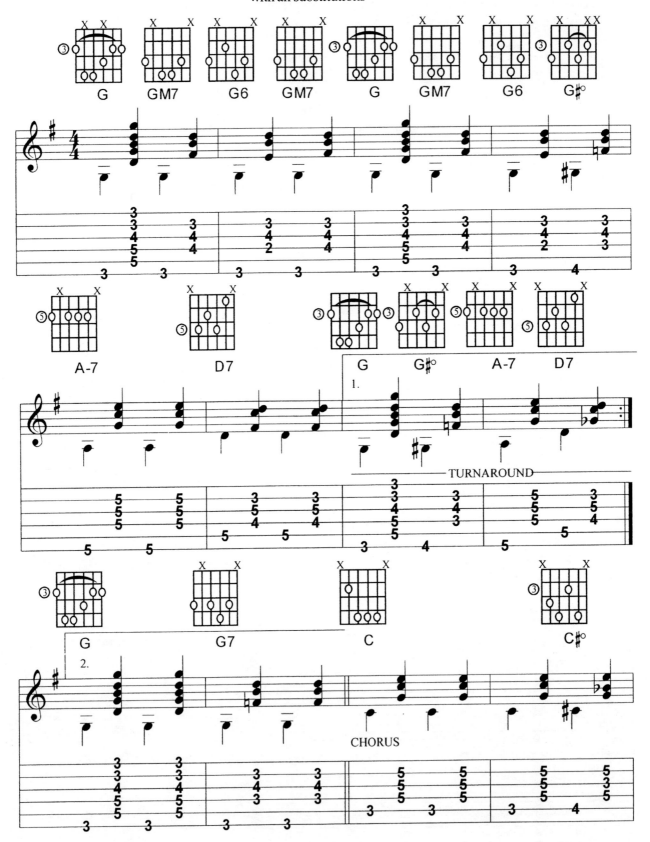

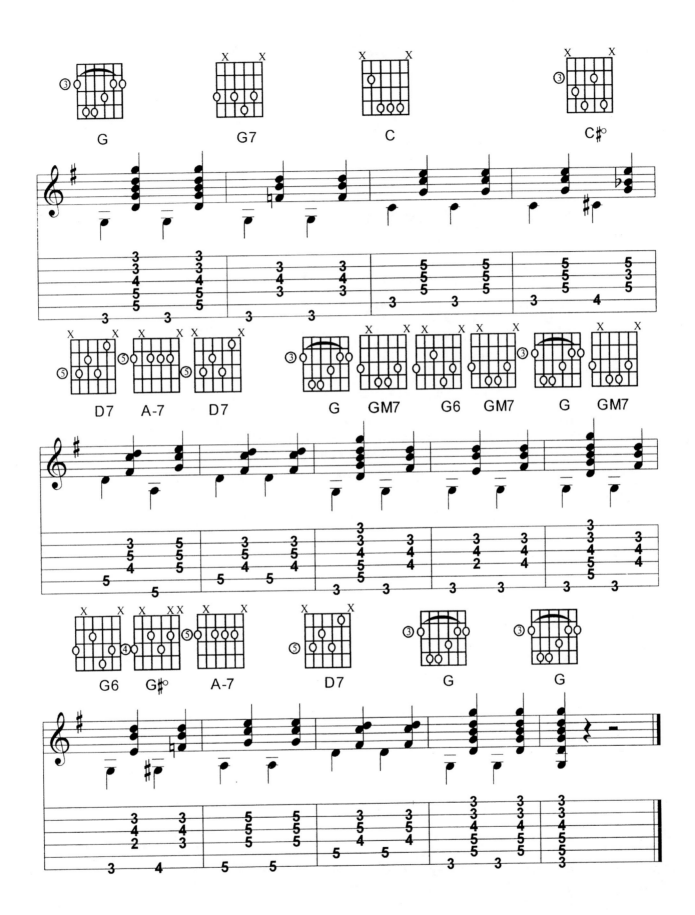

THREE NOTE CHORDS

Three note chord forms are popular with swing players and are used by Eldon and other great guitarists such as Freddie Green, who played for years with the Count Basie orchestra. These forms provide great moving harmonic sounds without getting in the way! Let's look at some of these forms. First we'll learn three major forms with the 1, 3, and 5 notes on the sixth string.

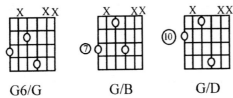

Notice that some three-note shapes can be two different chords.

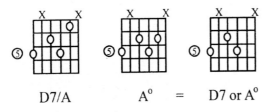

Practice moving from chord to chord with no hesitation. Mute the fifth string with the side of the finger that is fretting the sixth string. Be sure not to fret the fifth string. This technique takes a little getting used to, but it allows you to strum freely with your right hand. Also be sure to mute the first and second strings with the sides of your left hand fingers. Practice will reveal the exact techniques for your hand.

Now let's learn a simple progression in G that would work with a song like "Big Balls in Cowtown". The basic chart is:

G	G	C	G	or	1	1	4	1
G	G	D	G		1	1	5	1

(each chord worth 4 beats)

Here is an arrangement inspired by Eldon Shamblin. The arrangement starts with the G form at the seventh fret. Take some time to learn each new chord form. You will use them again.

COWTOWN

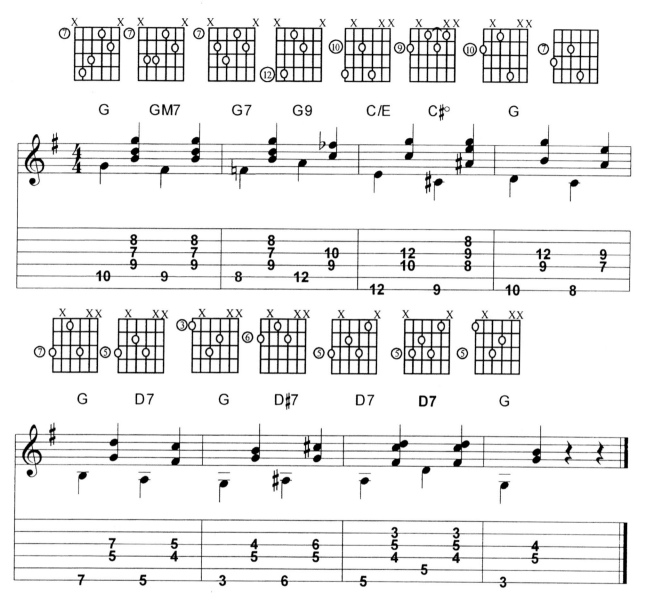

Use these two measures as a variation for the first 4 measures of "Cowtown."

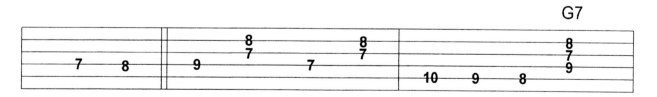

WESTPHALIA WALTZ

In a swing waltz rhythm, play the first beat followed by two shortened strums of the chord. This arrangement only features one new form, a useful inside string augmented chord.

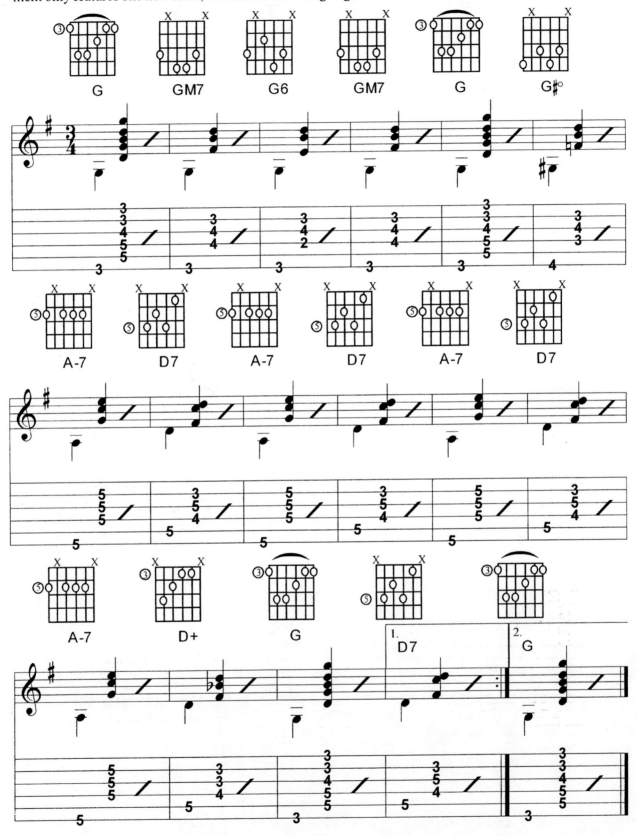

KIND OF LOVE

This next song is a medium ballad perfect for two stepping. Remember that swing music was to be danced to, so keep a strong rhythm pulse going even at slower tempos. The basic progression here is very simple.

1	1	1	1
5	5	1	1
1	1	1	1
5	5	1	1

Using magic substitution rules, the arrangement blossoms into this:

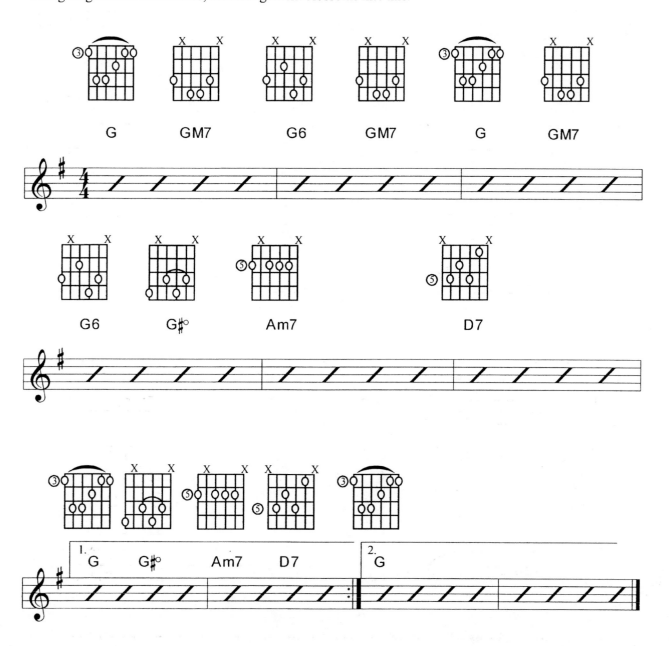

SAN ANTONIO RAG

Western swing guitaritsts sometimes connect their chords with single note bass note lines. It is amazing how effective these simple notes can be. This chord progression fits tunes like "Texas Playboy Rag" and "San Antonio Rose". Notice there are many muted strings in this arrangement. Strive for a clean sound.

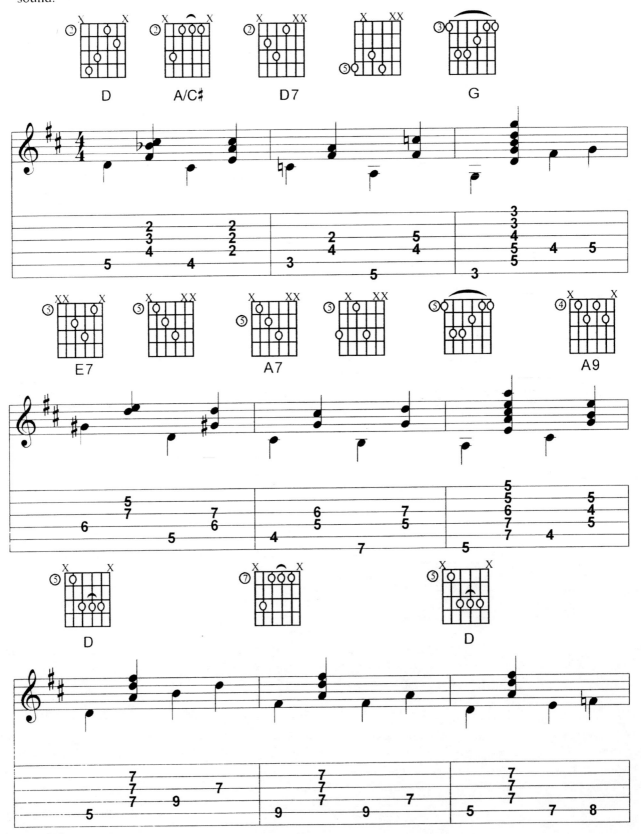

26

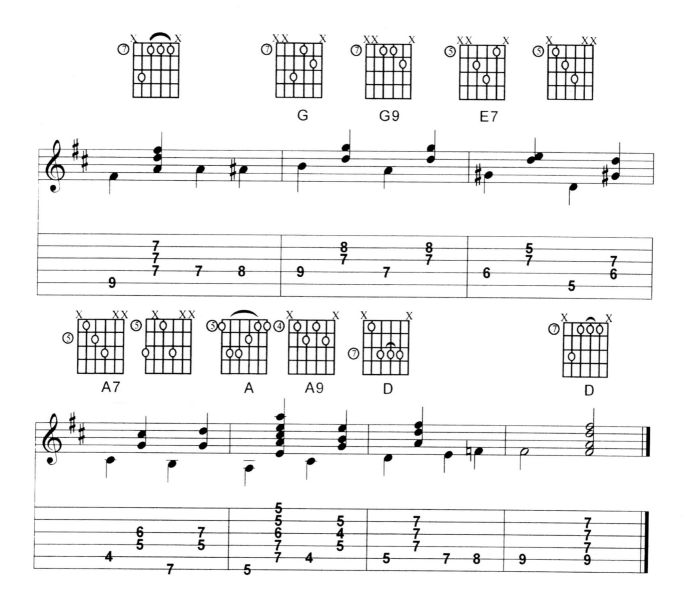

BALLAD IN F

Here is another ballad that fits the verse to a song like "Deep Water". Notice the use of the augmented chord to move from 1 to 4 (F to Bb). Also of interest is the descending bass line from G- to C9. This is a very popular move. Finally, notice the last measures and how the three-note form is used chromatically.

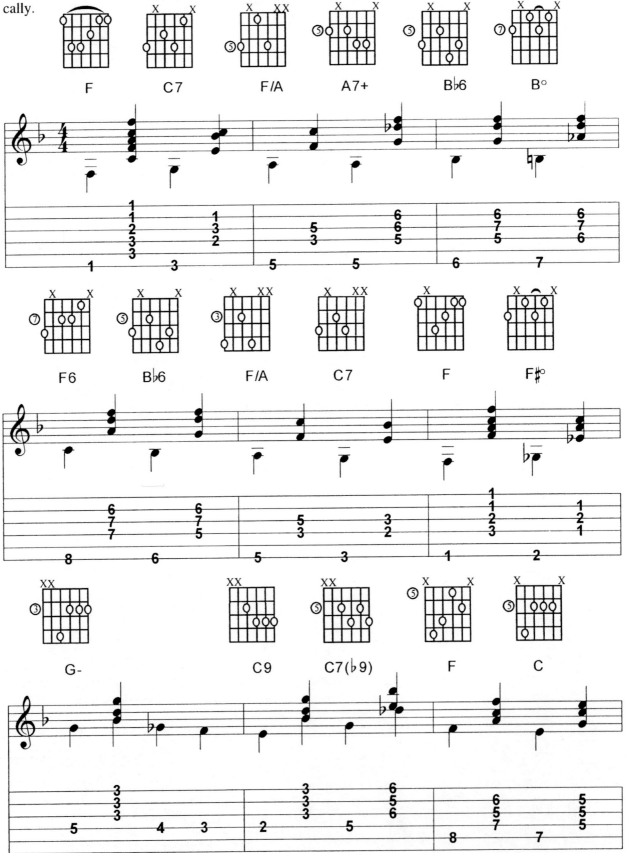

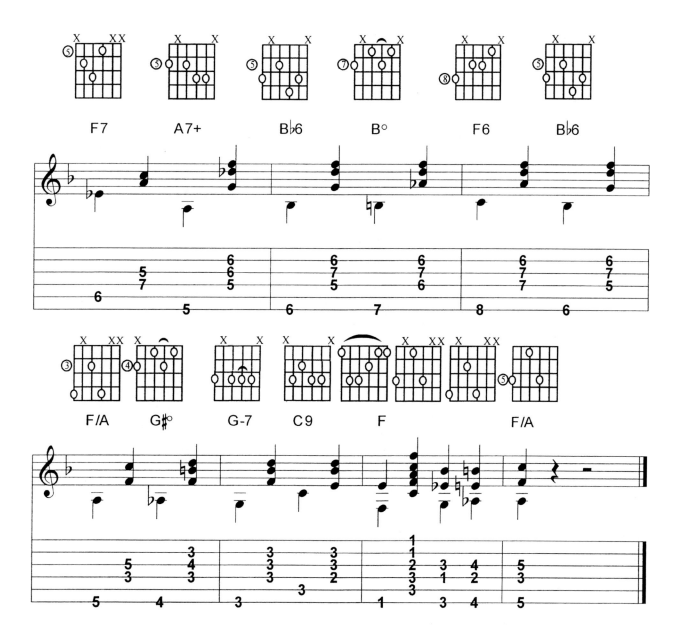

BLUES IN D

Here is our familiar blues in a new key and a new chord form. Ending 1 features a popular turnaround.
Expressed in numbers, it is: 1, #1°, 2-, 5. The descending pattern at the second ending moves to a 4
chord and the chords here get only one beat a piece. (B-7, B♭7, A-7, A♭7) In the beginning of the "B"
part of the song, we have a useful phase to use in a 4 to 1 situation, namely: 4, 4+, 2-, ♭3dim. Notice that
it creates an ascending chromatic line on the fifth string (very effective). Each frame is two beats unless
otherwise indicated.

IDA RED - ELDON STYLE

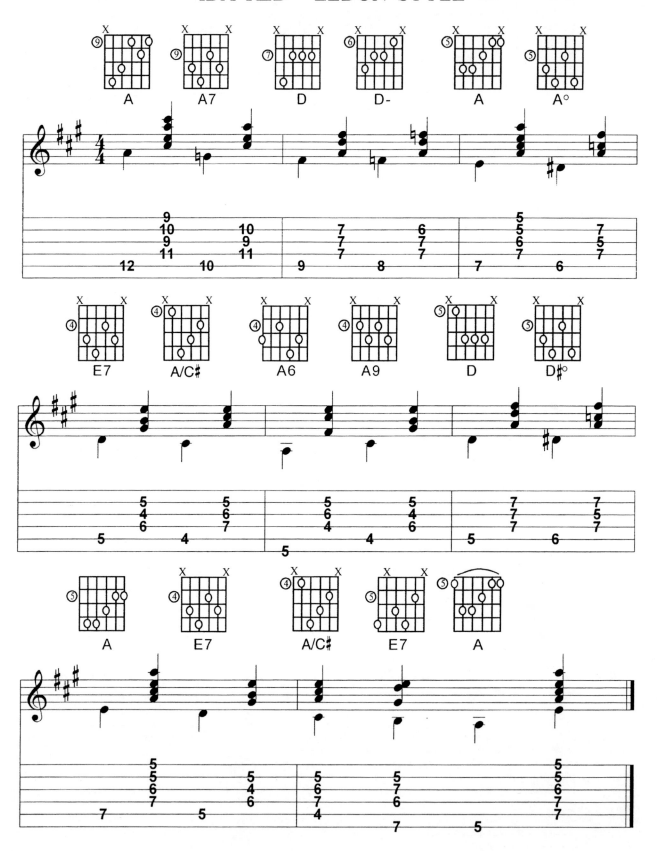

CORRINA

BEAUMONT RAG

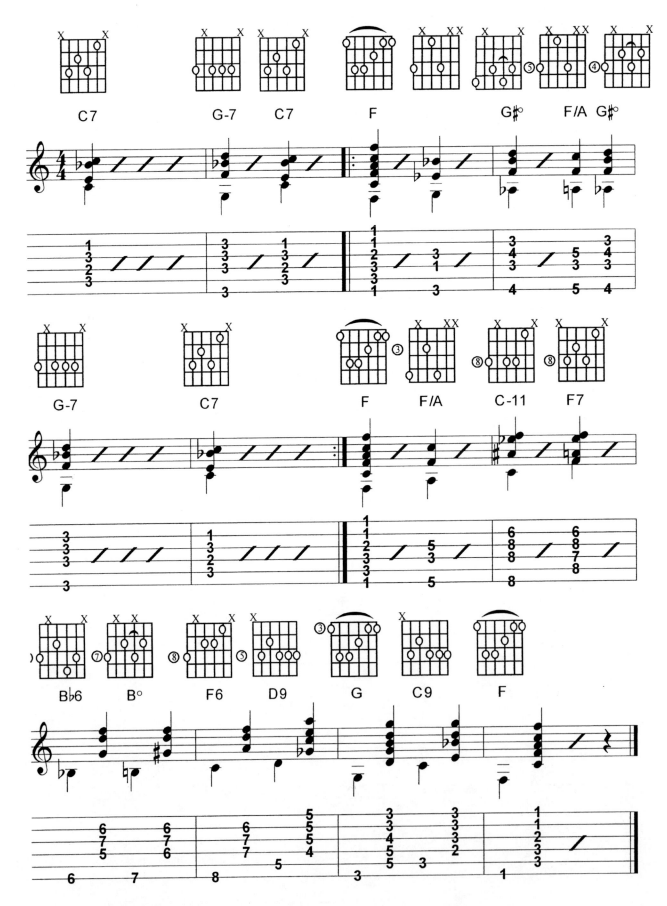

LILY

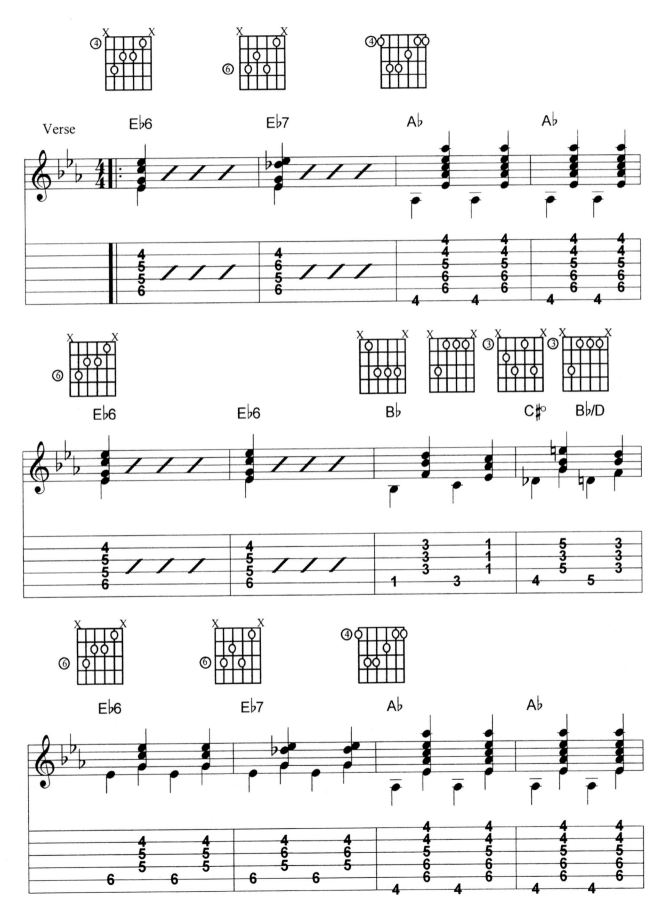

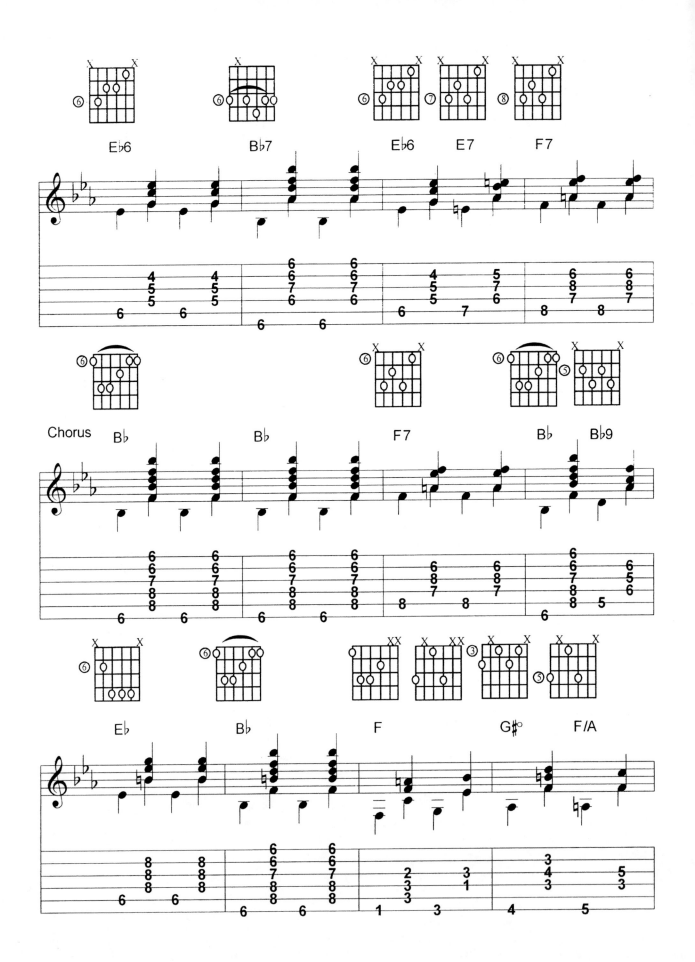

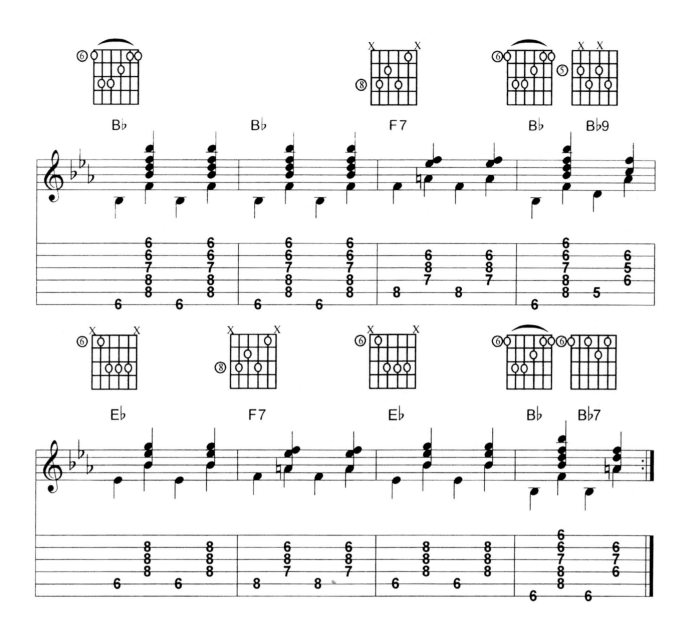

SUGAR

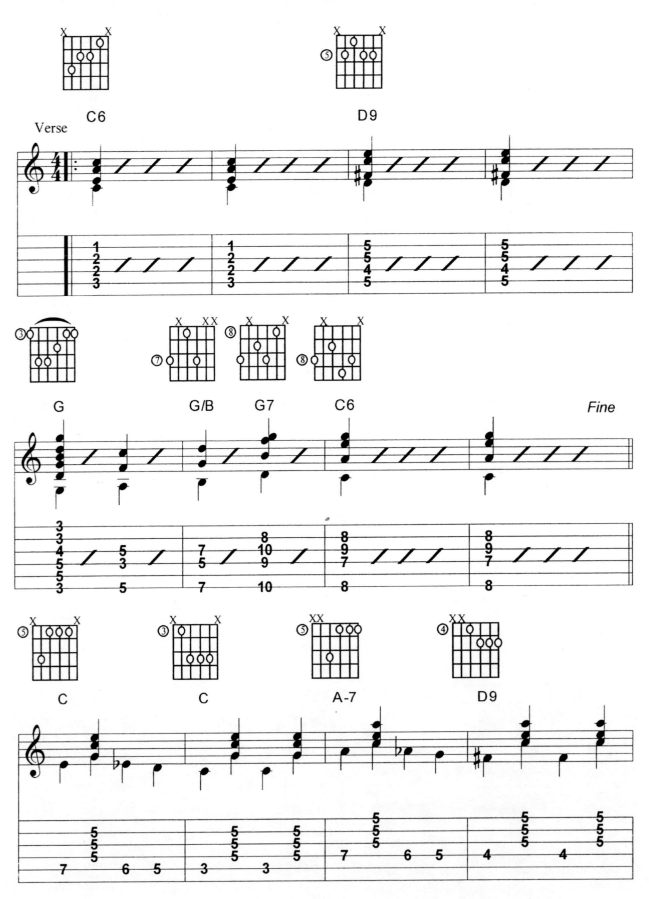

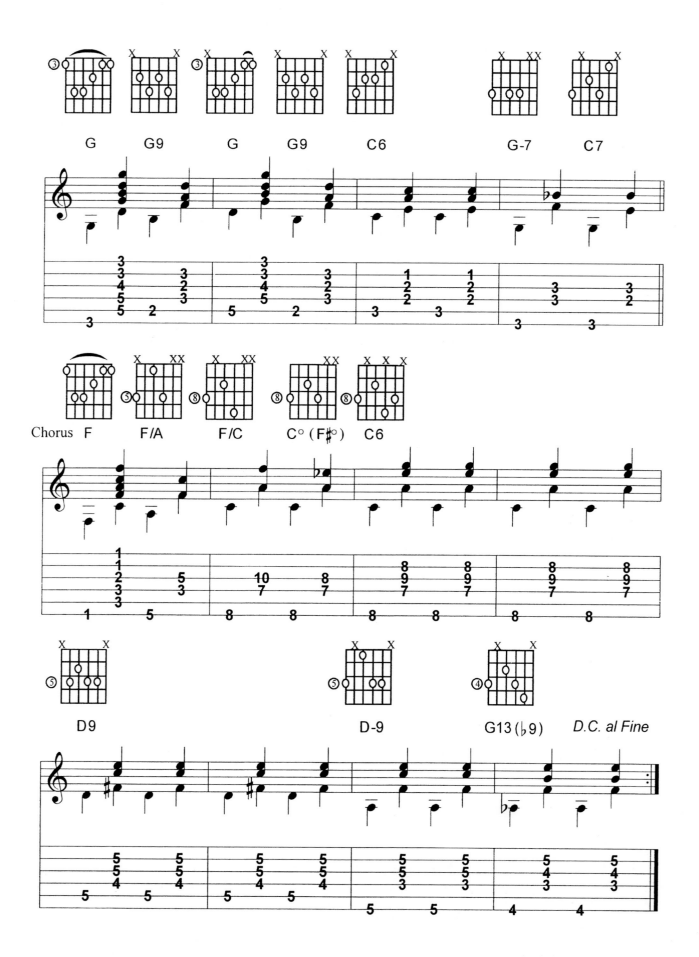

39

TIME / JUST A CLOSER

Try this progression with songs like "Time Changes Everything" or "Just a Closer Walk with Thee."

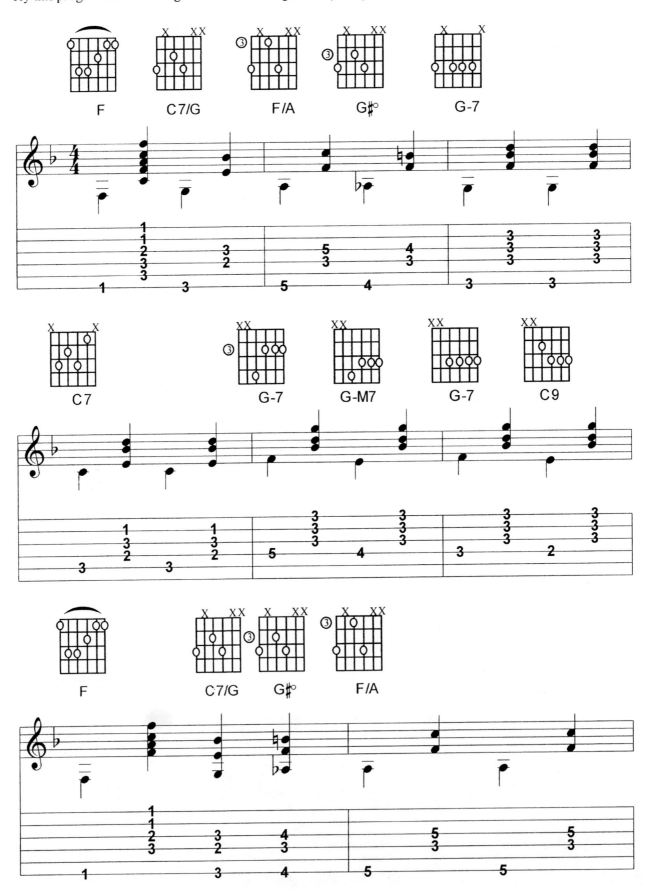

SOUTH

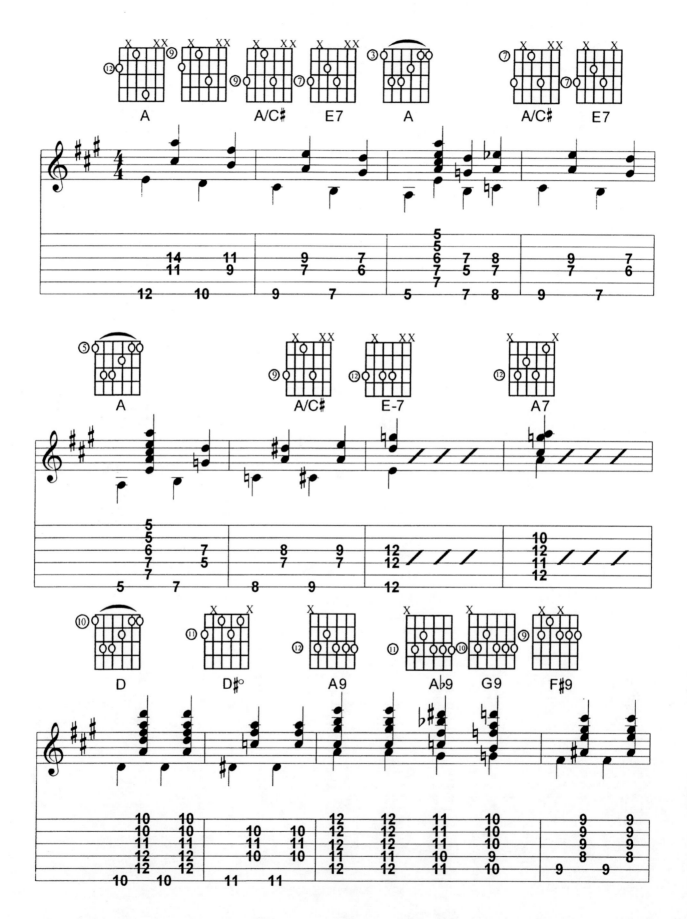

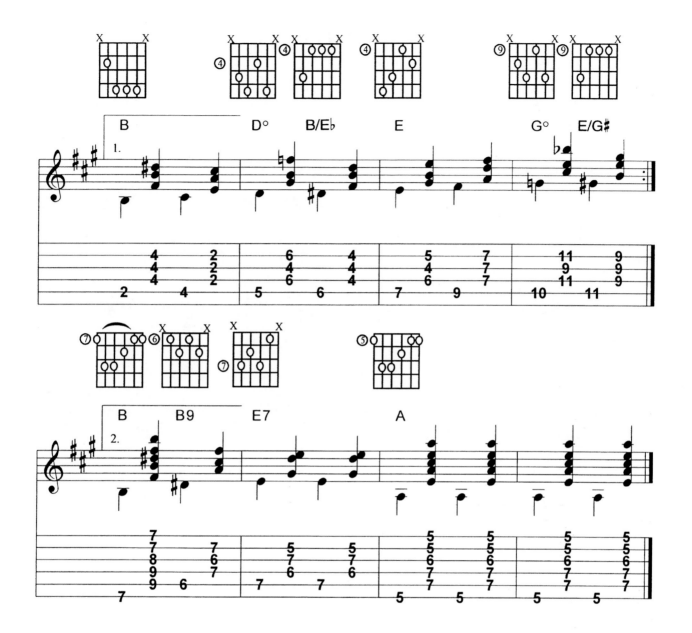

43

PIPELINE

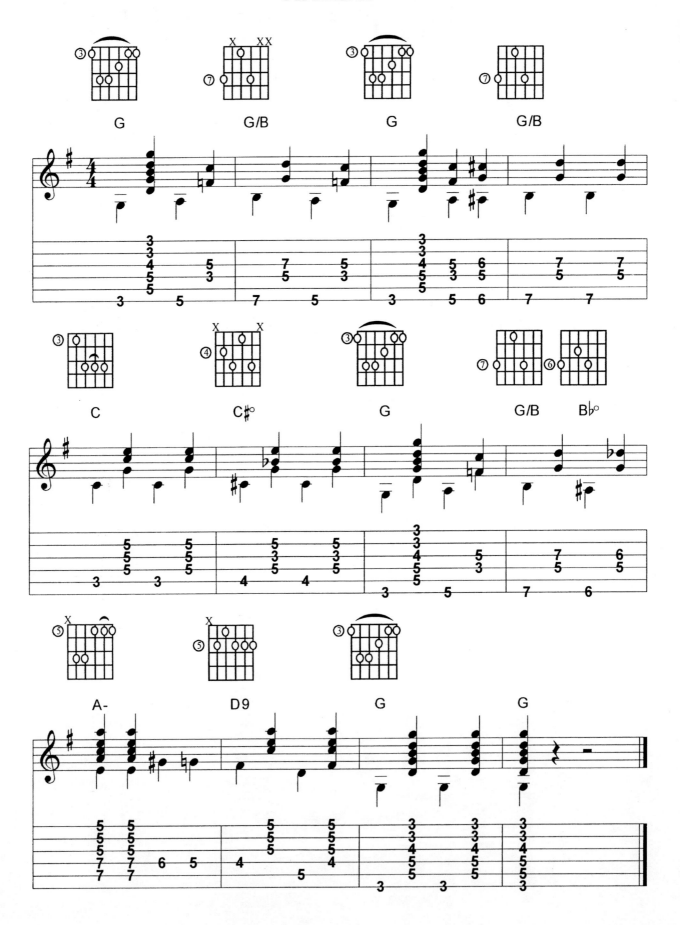

FINGERINGS FOR OPEN AND CLOSED POSITION CHORDS

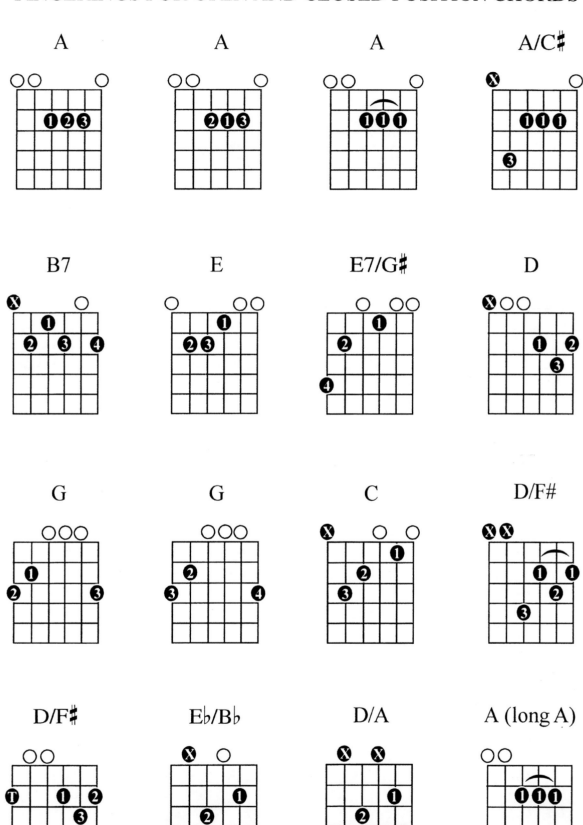

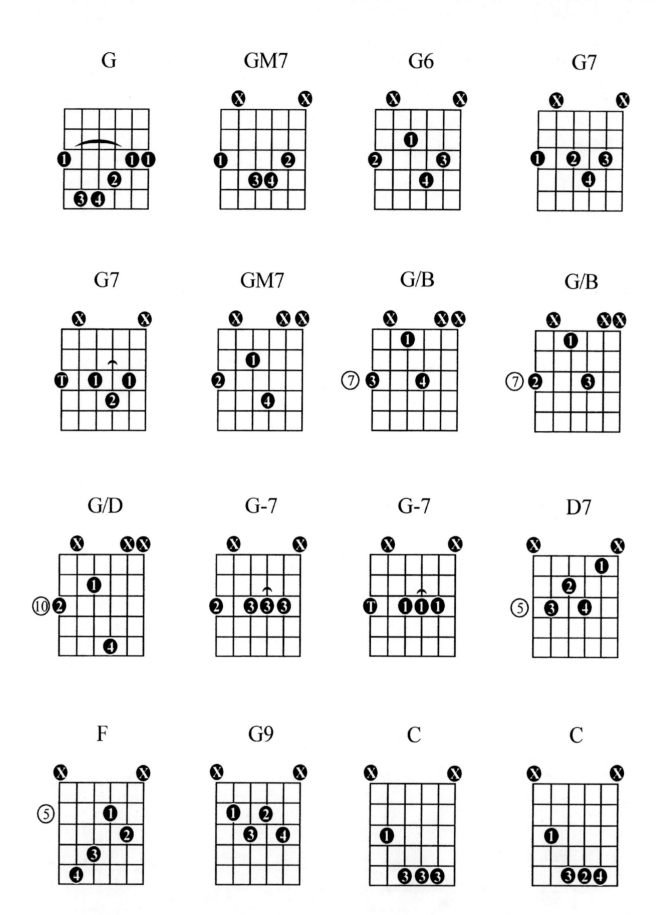

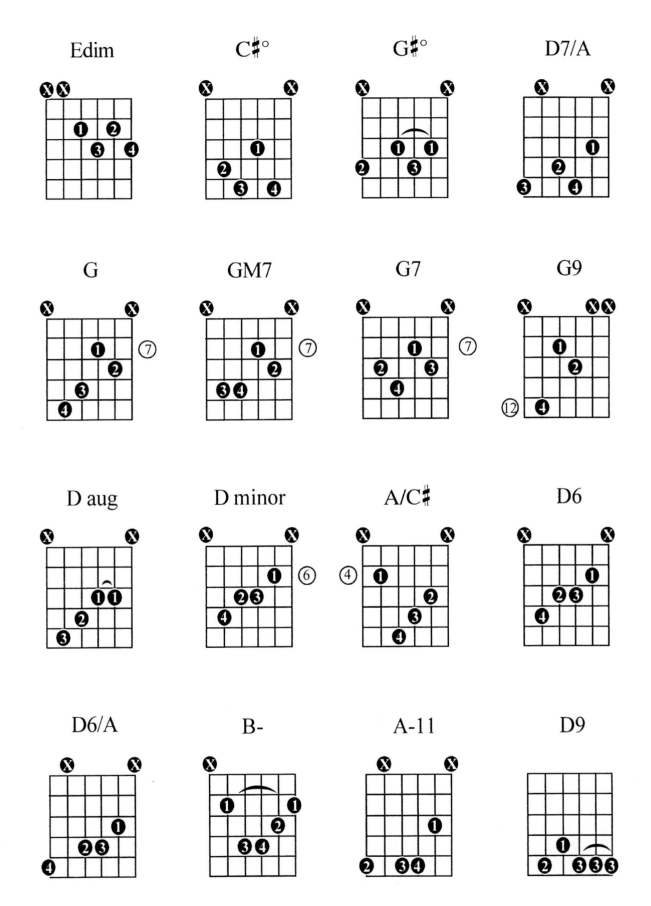

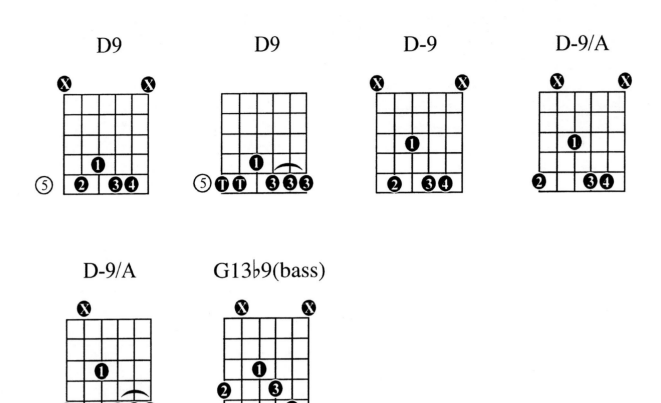

D9   D9   D-9   D-9/A

D-9/A   G13♭9(bass)

CONCLUSION

I hope this book sheds some light on the swing guitar rhythm. Take the ideas presented here and apply them to new songs and different keys. Once you have taken a musical concept and applied it in a new situation, you can truly call it your own.

JOE CARR

Guitar players may not recognize Joe Carr's name at first, but his face is probably familiar. That's because he appears in over twenty different instructional guitar videos ranging from country to western swing, bluegrass and even heavy metal! Add to these his videos on mandolin, fiddle, banjo and ukulele and Joe may be the most recorded video music instructor anywhere.

Joe is a self taught musician who started guitar at age 13. "My guitar heroes were the stars of the sixties, especially the folk musicians," recalls Carr. "One day, a high school friend played a Doc Watson record for me and flatpicking became my life."

Joe must have learned his lessons well. . . . a few years later he was hired to play guitar in Alan Munde's internationally known bluegrass group, COUNTRY GAZETTE. During the next six years Joe recorded three group albums, numerous sideman projects and produced his own critically acclaimed solo guitar album, "OTTER NONSENSE."

Joe left the Country Gazette in 1984 and joined the music faculty in the unique commercial music program at South Plains College in Levelland, Texas. Since then, he has worked with many young talented guitarists including the late Chris Austin of Reba McEntire's group, Ron Block with Allison Krauss and recording artist Heath Wright of RICOCHET.

Joe continues to perform nationally in a duo with former Gazette leader and South Plains College colleague, Alan Munde. "Alan and I have a great artistic communication that leads us into many new areas of music," Joe says. In addition to two albums on Flying Fish, Joe and Alan have completed a book about West Texas Country music called "Prairie Nights to Neon Lights" from the Texas Tech University Press.